SNIFFLE CRIME

VOL. 3: BOOK OF MURDER

TABLE OF CONTENTS

AUTHOR
DANIELA LINSBAUER

Daniela Linsbauer - a passionate dog trainer who keeps 2 dogs herself and is always on the lookout for new, active ideas for dog training.

The author was born in Vienna in 1985 and has always been an animal-loving person. Her name does not only stand for positive and non-violent dog training, but also for individual training: "Every dog learns in its own way and has different strengths and weaknesses".

Sniffing detective stories are very popular with dogs and owners, and dogs can show what they can do without being under pressure to perform. The author would like to make her written detective stories available to other dog trainers, so that the concept of "experience training" can spread, so that many dogs can enjoy it.

WHATS A SNIFFLE DETECTIVE STORY?

The sniffle detective story is very similar to a scavenger hunt and lasts about 3 hours. Man and dog have to work together and brood, sniff and combine - together a murder has to be determined. The dog sniffs out clues that form further puzzles for humans. Tasks have to be mastered together in order to get hold of further clues. The puzzles must be solved and witnesses questioned in order to find the motive and the murderer. Because the police are groping in the dark without the help of the sniff detectives....

The cooperation of man and dog is paramount, the playful nose work without pressure to perform, strengthens the bond between a dog and its owner. The fun and the common experience are the main focus. The dogs make their contribution with their nose and the people have to solve and combine puzzles. Some basic obedience is built in (running on a leash, etc.), working in a group is practiced - the training takes place unnoticed. You can also look at the sniffle detective story as a social walk.

The sniffer detectives with full commitment when sniffing out the clues

Schnüffel
KRIMINALFALL

The participants spend a few hours with their four-legged friends and with like-minded people. In the Crimean hike it doesn't matter who is the fastest or the best, it's the performance of the whole team that counts, and everyone contributes to it - be it by tracking down signs, displaying tracks or combining them logically. The participants also learn to read and trust their dog. Because the clever noses soon realize that they only have to follow the smell of the trainer. Because the trainer lays out the clues one hour beforehand.

In this casual ambience, relaxed conversations about the subject of dogs arise, forming friendships. The trainer is the organiser, but the participants take over the leading position.

The case can only be solved in a team, because time is running out.

PREPARATIONS

In this case a tour through a woodland is required. It is possible to find small clearings in between, where the tasks can be done afterwards.

The tour should not last longer than 30 - 45 minutes. The walks between the individual stations are important so that the dogs can calm down after the first excitement and the tension among the dogs is relaxed.

The sniffle detective story is announced about 1 month in advance. The duration of the detective story is about 3 hours. A detective story can be performed at any time of the year.

You can specify the conditions for participation in the invitation to participate:

- Since they work in a group, the dogs must be socially friendly.

- The dogs do not need any experience in man-trailing or tracking to participate. The detective stories are also suitable for beginners.

- Participating dogs must have liability insurance.

The participants need the following things to take part:

- 10-15m leash
- Chest harness
- Goodies
- Water
- Possibly clicker (for various exercises)

PREPARATIONS FOR THE DETECTIVE STORY

1. Sausage and cheese are cut into small pieces.

2. The cards are printed and wrapped.

3. Many small holes are made in small resealable plastic bags with the pin so that even beginners can smell the sausage well and find it.

4. The plastic bags are filled with the small cut goodies and the card that has been folded.

5. During this time, you fill bags with rivets ("Unfortunately no hint"). Even if the people don't get a hint, the dogs enjoy themselves after finding the sausage/ cheese. And the fun is the most important factor

6. You can also fill small pieces of paper into the plastic bags with the note "No poison, please leave it there". Since a lot of poison is currently being spread out, another dog owner should not have a heart attack because his dog has found sausage and eaten it.

7. Every detective story has a specific theme: Here it is about Impulse control. You are free to supplement or exchange the exercises so that it remains exciting.

8. Prepare a detective pass for each participant. This is a small detail that is very well received. The detectives then have to present this ID during interviews etc.

An example of a detective badge

9. You can print a map of the area you want to work in on Google Maps. Here you draw the individual places where you have hidden clues for the participants. The map will then be handed over to a clerk.

map sample

10. You have to lay out the filled plastic bags about 1 hour before the detective story. Stick to your route and don't hide the bags where it will be too difficult for beginners. Hollow trees, tree roots, under bushes or in holes on the ground are particularly suitable.

11. For each story, a clerk is selected to collect all the clues in a plastic bag. He also receives the map, notes and pencil so that the participants can take notes.

Additional preparations:

- Prepare a dummy or a treat dummy for the exercises

- Laminate and cut out the 2 puzzles

- Prepare the math exercises

Rambo found a well-hidden clue.

PROCEDURE

Not only participants with a dog, but also accompanying persons without a dog take part in a sniffing detective story. Therefore, you should prepare puzzles in which the companions can take part, so that they don't get bored.

Please keep in mind that you always have an emergency plan. Because it can repeatedly occur that not all clues are found. Because they have been found and eaten by other walking dogs, for example. An emergency plan can be e.g.: an additionally prepared puzzle or you tell the participants the lost clues just like that.

Price suggestion: between 45 - 55 Euro per person/ dog team and approx. 20 - 25 Euro per accompanying person

Leo found a clue and is waiting for his reward.

Schnüffel
KRIMINALFALL

ROUND OF INTERVIEWS

At the beginning of the detective story you introduce the case and ask all participants to introduce themselves and their dogs. This is important for everyone involved, especially if there is an anxious dog among the puzzlers who doesn't like other dogs getting too close.

This is followed by a discussion of the detective story and some basic rules, such as

- Please take your dog back if he has already found 2 bags at one station and give the other participants the chance to find something.

- If a dog has found a clue, please do not let your dog go to the four-legged friend waiting for food. This could lead to a dispute.

- Please keep your dogs on a leash at all times.

- It is normal that dogs who participate for the first time need a little time to understand what this is all about. Give them the time or help them with the search at the beginning.

CRIME START

At the beginning of the detective story, you choose a clerk. He should collect all the clues and read them aloud. He also receives the map and thus determines the path.

Then the team works - all dogs and people start together and solve the case together. If a dog is tired and wants to take a break, that's fine. All results are always read aloud. Please always wait until all participants are together.

Doti takes a little break after completing her task.

BOOK OF MURDER

Announcement and Introduction of the Crime Story:

„A tragedy: The famous author Richard Nebelhaus was found dead and fully covered in blood in a remote mountain cabin. The police is completely in the dark regarding the strange circumstances of his passing.

Who would have wanted the successful writer dead? Many were jealous of Richard so the list of suspects is long... There are questions over questions that need to be answered."

The body has already been transferred to the coroner's office and we are waiting on the forensic report. In the meantime, the police has cleared the crime scene for us. We should start there.

1ST STATION: VICTIM AND FORENSIC REPORT

6 yellow cards

- Richard Nebelhaus was struck dead with a log of wood
- The victim had large wounds on the back of the head, the forehead and the temple
- The cabin clearly shows signs of a struggle. Richard tried to fight off his killer
- The latest crime novel, that Richard was working on, was stolen
- Richard has been dead for 10 days already
- All valuables and money were left behin

Who had any idea that Richard was staying in the mountain cabin? Did Richard tell anyone? Obviously, the murderer had the intension to steal Richard's latest book, which the author was not going to give up voluntarily. Is that why he had to die?

We have to investigate further.

Vanilla is eagerly looking for clues

Sniffle CRIME

2ND STATION: CIRCUMSTANCES AND SUSPECTS

7 teal cards

Do not hide all of the clues. Keep 1-2 of the cards with you. In order to earn those, the participants and their dogs have to solve the following challenges:

Hide a **treat dummy** which the dogs must find and retrieve. During the summer you can incorporate the dogs fetching it from **the water**.

If every dog found the dummy at least once, the team receives the last clue.

Sarah loves fetching the dummy and earns further clues with it

- Richard is single and has a 32-year-old son from his first marriage, named Rafael
- 5 weeks ago the victim retreated to the remote cabin to finish his latest crime novel
- Richard does not have a lot of contact with his son Rafael
- The victim was known to be hardheaded, easily confused and often withdrawn
- Richard has no family, no siblings
- The author only has one close friend: the restaurant's owner Hannes Pflügl
- Richards's crime novels are always based on a tiny little bit of truth. That's why they are so successful

We should find out who the suspects are and what their motives could be. We need to continue our investigation.

Schnüffel
KRIMINALFALL

3RD STATION: SUSPECTS

6 blue cards

Zoe and Missy found some clues and are now allowed to eat the treats.

The rules are the same. Again, don't hide one of the clues. The participants have to work to earn it. Every dog is paired up with a person. The team needs to demonstrate that it knows the basic obedience commands, such as SIT, DOWN, STAY and COME. If everyone in the team succeeds, the next clue will be revealed.

- Richard's son resents his father, because he walked out on him and his mother years ago
- Richard's ex-wife has psychological problems and has been in therapy for years.
- Richard's ex-wife does not have anything good to say about him. She claims that she only started having mental problems once he left her.
- The author has one big competitor: Markus Wilming, who loves stealing his ideas or copying them
- The victim wasn't very well liked in the town he lived in due to his bizarre behavior.
- Richard was always picking fights with everyone, hence he didn't have many friends.

Obviously, Richard was not very popular and there are countless people who would have a motive for his murder. Maybe we have to dig even deeper to get closer to solving the case.

Sniffle CRIME

4TH STATION

Puzzle Pieces

A page from the missing crime novel, smeared with blood and dirt, has been found. But it was torn to pieces. Looks like the participants must put the puzzle pieces back together in order to learn what is written on the page.

In the story, a mentally ill ex-wife is stalking her ex-husband

> That sounds exactly like Richard's life ... As we've already learned, Richard's books are always based on a little bit of truth. And the mentally ill ex-wife does exist in reality. Maybe she wanted to prevent the publication and has therefore killed the author and stolen the book...? What is your theory?

Chester is waiting for his treat for finding the hint

Schnüffel
KRIMINALFALL

5TH STATION: MATH PROBLEMS AND PHONE NUMBER

The participants must solve several math problems. The numbers from the answers make up a phone number that the participants must call. An anonymous tip was previously recorded under the phone number.

„Richard has another son. He was born outside of his marriage and up until recently Richard didn't even know anything about him. A photo of him has been submitted to the police already." The photo was also forwarded to us.

Show the photo to the group.

Richard's illegitimate son

This case is getting more complicated by the minute. We have to find out if the suspects have an alibi and verify it.

6TH STATION: ALIBIS

5 green cards

- Richard's ex-wife was in a mental institution when the murder took place.
- On the day of the murder Richard's ex-wife was on leave
- Richard's son Rafael was travelling abroad for business
- Rafael's business trip can be confirmed with the airline.
- Markus Wilming, Richard's biggest competition, was on a book tour to introduce his latest book.

The investigation is a lot of fun for the dogs.

This truly is a mysterious case. Is Verena behind the murder? We should take a look around at the facility where she is institutionalized. And does the ominous son really exist?

7TH STATION

5 red cards

- Recently Verena had a lot of visits by a person whose identity is unknown.

- She was prescribed stronger medication due to the fact that she still firmly believed that Richard and her were a couple.

- During her drugged-out haze she stated that Richard needed to be warned.

- Verena was clearly still in love with Richard.

- The patient was in denial about the breakup with Richard

Is Verena really the person behind the murder? Who is the mysterious stranger? I will ask the police for the security camera tape. If we can get the footage of the visits, that may shed some light on the stranger's identity...

Schoko is looking for more hints

8TH STATION

Puzzle Pieces

The dogs have to find a photo puzzle of the mysterious stranger. The participants have to put the puzzle together.

Answer: The unknown man, who was making frequent visits to Richard's ex-wife is his illegitimate son.

Putting the puzzle back together is teamwork.

Case solved:

Richard's illegitimate son went to see him and asked him to publicly admit that he is his father. Richard declined and that's when the fight broke out. The rejected son struck him down out of anger and desperation.

But before that he sought out Richard's ex in order to find out more about his father.

The completed book was taken in order to cover up the murder and lead investigators down the wrong path.

Schnüffel **KRIMINALFALL**

ATTACHEMENTS

MATH EXERCISES

1) 98615522,4:16435920,4 = ?
   Solution= 6

2) Which is the 32nd decimal place of π after the decimal point?
   Answer: 0

3) 15+8:(6*3-16)*(3+5-4)-(3*5-10)-(-19+6*6)= ?
   Solution = 9

4) 36km/h =? m/s
   Solution: 10m/s

5) 0,0625 = 1/x
   Solution: x=16

6) At what digit is 256 at a power of 2?
   Solution: 8

7) Two roofages with 5x7m each should be covered with tiles. The architect says that he needs to use
   10 tiles per m². The customer pays with:
    8 x 500 Euro bills
    4 x 200 Euro bills
   10 x 50 Euro bills
   How much is one tile?
   Answer: 7

8) It is 2012. The Olympic Games in London. You participate in the 100-meter dash. It's the third day
   of the games, the time is 14:30 and it's 31°C. You start in the fourth run. After 4 seconds you take
   over the runner-up and you keep that position. Which place did you reach?
   Answer: 2

9) 15+8:(6*3-16)*(3+5-4)-(3*5*10)-(-19+6-6)=?
   Solution = 9

10) How many sides does a tetrahedron have?
    Answer: 4

11) In which quadrant of the coordinate system is 210° positioned??
    Answer: 3

12) 518400 seconds = ? days
    Answer: 6

13) A pool has a size of 6x4m and is 2.5m deep. How many cubic meters does it have?
    Answer: 60

14) $$\frac{10^3 - 10^2 + 10^4 - 10^1 - 8*10^2 - 9*10^2}{5*10^3} = ?$$ Solution = 2

15) $c = ?$ $b = 4cm$ Solution: c=5
      $a = 3cm$

16) $$\frac{R*B - (a+b)*N + B*N + (a+b) + N}{B*R - 2*(x+y) - (a+b) - 2} = 5$$

    (a+b) = 5 = R
    (x+y) = 4 = B
    (c+d) = 2 = N

17) $$\frac{(^{625}/_{5} - 100 + ^{20}/_{10}) * 6F}{^{3600}/_{600}} = 6$$

Schnüffel
KRIMINALFALL

ATTACHMENT CRIME NOVEL

Please laminate and cut into puzzle pieces

[text heavily obscured by ink splatters]

... A mentally ill woman was stalking him ...

... afraid, because this woman was dangerous and not to be trusted. ...

... Nobody believed him because the woman ... harmless ...

Schnüffel
KRIMINALFALL

ATTACHEMENT CARDS

Please laminate and cut out

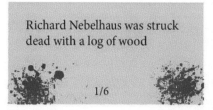

Richard Nebelhaus was struck dead with a log of wood

1/6

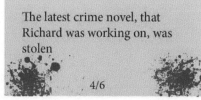

The latest crime novel, that Richard was working on, was stolen

4/6

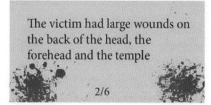

The victim had large wounds on the back of the head, the forehead and the temple

2/6

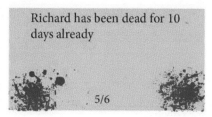

Richard has been dead for 10 days already

5/6

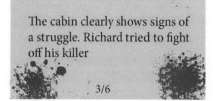

The cabin clearly shows signs of a struggle. Richard tried to fight off his killer

3/6

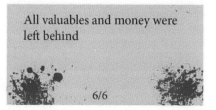

All valuables and money were left behind

6/6

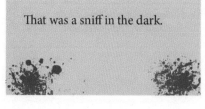

That was a sniff in the dark.

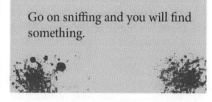

Go on sniffing and you will find something.

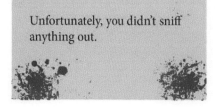

Unfortunately, you didn't sniff anything out.

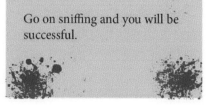

Go on sniffing and you will be successful.

Schnüffel KRIMINALFALL

Richard is single and has a 32-year-old son from his first marriage, named Rafael

1/7

Richard has no family and no siblings

2/7

5 weeks ago the victim retreated to the remote cabin to finish his latest crime novel

3/7

The author only has one close friend: the restaurant's owner Hannes Pflügl

4/7

Richard does not have a lot of contact with his son Rafael

5/7

Richards's crime novels are always based on a tiny little bit of truth. That's why they are so successful

6/7

The victim was known to be hardheaded, easily confused and often withdrawn

7/7

That was a sniff in the dark.

Go on sniffing and you will find something.

Unfortunately, you didn't sniff anything out.

Go on sniffing and you will be successful.

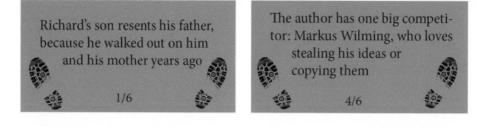

Richard's son resents his father, because he walked out on him and his mother years ago

1/6

The author has one big competitor: Markus Wilming, who loves stealing his ideas or copying them

4/6

Richard's ex-wife has psychological problems and has been in therapy for years.

2/6

The victim wasn't very well liked in the town he lived in due to his bizarre behavior.

5/6

Richard's ex-wife claims that she only started having mental problems once he left her.

3/6

Richard was always picking fights with everyone, hence he didn't have many friends.

6/6

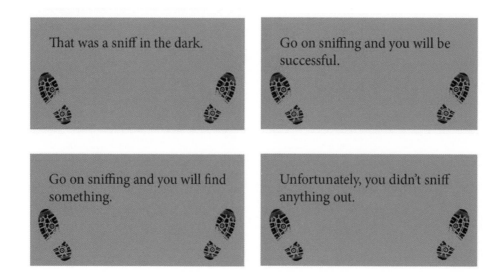

That was a sniff in the dark.

Go on sniffing and you will be successful.

Go on sniffing and you will find something.

Unfortunately, you didn't sniff anything out.

Schnüffel
KRIMINALFALL

Recently Verena had a lot of visits by a person whose identity is unknown.

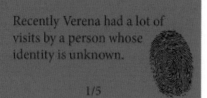

1/5

Verena was clearly still in love with Richard.

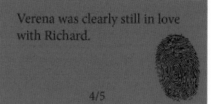

4/5

She was prescribed stronger medication due to the fact that she still firmly believed that Richard and her were a couple.

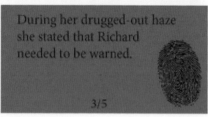

2/5

The patient was in denial about the breakup with Richard

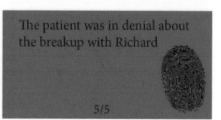

5/5

During her drugged-out haze she stated that Richard needed to be warned.

3/5

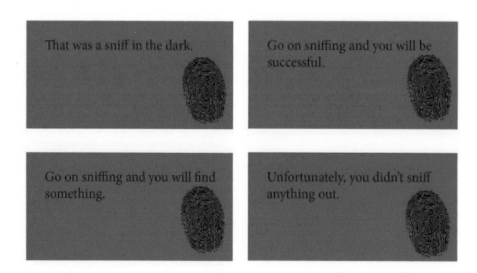

That was a sniff in the dark.

Go on sniffing and you will be successful.

Go on sniffing and you will find something.

Unfortunately, you didn't sniff anything out.

Schnüffel
KRIMINALFALL

Richard's ex-wife was in a mental institution when the murder took place.

1/5

On the day of the murder Richard's ex-wife was on leave

2/5

Richard's son Rafael was travelling abroad for business

3/5

Rafael's business trip can be confirmed with the airline.

4/5

Markus Wilming, Richard's biggest competition, was on a book tour to introduce his late book.

5/5

That was a sniff in the dark.

Go on sniffing and you will be successful.

Go on sniffing and you will find something.

Unfortunately, you didn't sniff anything out.

ID'S

Please fill in names, laminate and cut out

Badge number.: 08990

_____

_____

with a license to sniff

certified

Badge number.: 08994

_____

_____

with a license to sniff

certified

Badge number.: 08991

_____

_____

with a license to sniff

certified

Badge number.: 08995

_____

_____

with a license to sniff

certified

Badge number.: 08992

_____

_____

with a license to sniff

certified

Badge number.: 08996

_____

_____

with a license to sniff

certified

Badge number.: 08993

_____

_____

with a license to sniff

certified

Badge number.: 08997

_____

_____

with a license to sniff

certified

Schnüffel KRIMINALFALL

ATTACHEMENT PHOTO OF RICHARDS SON, BORN OUT OF WEDLOCK

Please laminate and cut out

ATTACHEMENT PUZZLE

Please laminate and cut into pieces

Schnüffel
KRIMINALFALL

MATH EXERCISES

1) 98615522,4:16435920,4 = ?
   Solution= 6

2) Which is the 32nd decimal place of π after the decimal point?
   Answer: 0

3) 15+8:(6*3-16)*(3+5-4)-(3*5-10)-(-19+6*6)= ?
   Solution = 9

4) 36km/h =? m/s
   Solution: 10m/s

5) 0,0625 = 1/x
   Solution: x=16

6) At what digit is 256 at a power of 2?
   Solution: 8

7) Two roofages with 5x7m each should be covered with tiles. The architect says that he needs to use
   10 tiles per m². The customer pays with:
   8 x 500 Euro bills
   4 x 200 Euro bills
   10 x 50 Euro bills
   How much is one tile?
   Answer: 7

8) It is 2012. The Olympic Games in London. You participate in the 100-meter dash. It's the third day
   of the games, the time is 14:30 and it's 31°C. You start in the fourth run. After 4 seconds you take
   over the runner-up and you keep that position. Which place did you reach?
   Answer: 2

9) 15+8:(6*3-16)*(3+5-4)-(3*5*10)-(-19+6-6)=?
   Solution = 9

10) How many sides does a tetrahedron have?
    Answer: 4

11) In which quadrant of the coordinate system is 210° positioned??
    Answer: 3

12) 518400 seconds = ? days
    Answer: 6

13) A pool has a size of 6x4m and is 2.5m deep. How many cubic meters does it have?
    Answer: 60

14) $\dfrac{10^3 - 10^2 + 10^4 - 10^1 - 8*10^2 - 9*10^2}{5*10^3}$ = ?   Solution = 2

15)

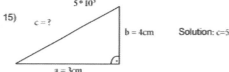

c = ?   b = 4cm   Solution: c=5
a = 3cm

16) $\dfrac{R*B - (a+b)*N + B*N + (a+b) + N}{B*R - 2*(x+y) - (a+b) - 2}$ = 5

   (a+b) = 5 = R
   (x+y) = 4 = B
   (c+d) = 2 = N

17) $\dfrac{(^{625}/_{\%} - 100 + ^{20}/_{10}) *6F}{^{3600}/_{600}}$ = 6

Schnüffel
KRIMINALFALL

ATTACHMENT CRIME NOVEL

Please laminate and cut into puzzle pieces

[text obscured by ink]

... A mentally ill woman was stalking him.

... afraid, because this woman was dangerous and not to be trusted. ...

... Nobody believed him because the woman ...

Schnüffel KRIMINALFALL

ATTACHEMENT CARDS

Please laminate and cut out

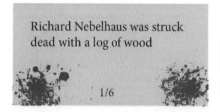

Richard Nebelhaus was struck dead with a log of wood

1/6

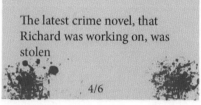

The latest crime novel, that Richard was working on, was stolen

4/6

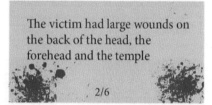

The victim had large wounds on the back of the head, the forehead and the temple

2/6

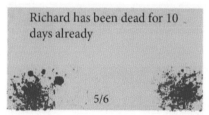

Richard has been dead for 10 days already

5/6

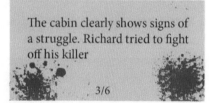

The cabin clearly shows signs of a struggle. Richard tried to fight off his killer

3/6

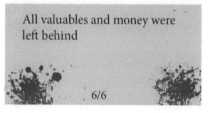

All valuables and money were left behind

6/6

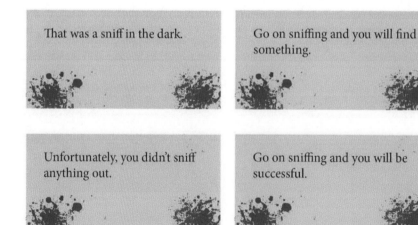

That was a sniff in the dark.

Go on sniffing and you will find something.

Unfortunately, you didn't sniff anything out.

Go on sniffing and you will be successful.

Schnüffel
KRIMINALFALL

Richard is single and has a 32-year-old son from his first marriage, named Rafael

1/7

Richard has no family and no siblings

2/7

5 weeks ago the victim retreated to the remote cabin to finish his latest crime novel

3/7

The author only has one close friend: the restaurant's owner Hannes Pflügl

4/7

Richard does not have a lot of contact with his son Rafael

5/7

Richards's crime novels are always based on a tiny little bit of truth. That's why they are so successful

6/7

The victim was known to be hardheaded, easily confused and often withdrawn

7/7

That was a sniff in the dark.

Go on sniffing and you will find something.

Unfortunately, you didn't sniff anything out.

Go on sniffing and you will be successful.

Richard's son resents his father, because he walked out on him and his mother years ago

1/6

The author has one big competitor: Markus Wilming, who loves stealing his ideas or copying them

4/6

Richard's ex-wife has psychological problems and has been in therapy for years.

2/6

The victim wasn't very well liked in the town he lived in due to his bizarre behavior.

5/6

Richard's ex-wife claims that she only started having mental problems once he left her.

3/6

Richard was always picking fights with everyone, hence he didn't have many friends.

6/6

That was a sniff in the dark.

Go on sniffing and you will be successful.

Go on sniffing and you will find something.

Unfortunately, you didn't sniff anything out.

Recently Verena had a lot of visits by a person whose identity is unknown.

1/5

Verena was clearly still in love with Richard.

4/5

She was prescribed stronger medication due to the fact that she still firmly believed that Richard and her were a couple.

2/5

The patient was in denial about the breakup with Richard

5/5

During her drugged-out haze she stated that Richard needed to be warned.

3/5

That was a sniff in the dark.

Go on sniffing and you will be successful.

Go on sniffing and you will find something.

Unfortunately, you didn't sniff anything out.

Schnüffel
KRIMINALFALL

Richard's ex-wife was in a mental institution when the murder took place.

1/5

Rafael's business trip can be confirmed with the airline.

4/5

On the day of the murder Richard's ex-wife was on leave

2/5

Markus Wilming, Richard's biggest competition, was on a book tour to introduce his latest book.

5/5

Richard's son Rafael was travelling abroad for business

3/5

That was a sniff in the dark.

Go on sniffing and you will be successful.

Go on sniffing and you will find something.

Unfortunately, you didn't sniff anything out.

Schnüffel
KRIMINALFALL

ID'S

Please fill in names, laminate and cut out

Badge number.: 08990

_____

_____

with a license to sniff

Badge number.: 08994

_____

_____

with a license to sniff

Badge number.: 08991

_____

_____

with a license to sniff

Badge number.: 08995

_____

_____

with a license to sniff

Badge number.: 08992

_____

_____

with a license to sniff

Badge number.: 08996

_____

_____

with a license to sniff

Badge number.: 08993

_____

_____

with a license to sniff

Badge number.: 08997

_____

_____

with a license to sniff

Schnüffel **KRIMINALFALL**

ATTACHEMENT PHOTO OF RICHARDS SON, BORN OUT OF WEDLOCK

Please laminate and cut out

ATTACHEMENT PUZZLE

Please laminate and cut into pieces

Schnüffel
KRIMINALFALL

MATH EXERCISES

1) 98615522,4:16435920,4 = ?
Solution= 6

2) Which is the 32nd decimal place of π after the decimal point?
Answer: 0

3) 15+8:(6*3-16)*(3+5-4)-(3*5-10)-(-19+6*6)= ?
Solution = 9

4) 36km/h =? m/s
Solution: 10m/s

5) 0,0625 = 1/x
Solution: x=16

6) At what digit is 256 at a power of 2?
Solution: 8

7) Two roofages with 5x7m each should be covered with tiles. The architect says that he needs to use 10 tiles per m². The customer pays with:
8 x 500 Euro bills
4 x 200 Euro bills
10 x 50 Euro bills
How much is one tile?
Answer: 7

8) It is 2012. The Olympic Games in London. You participate in the 100-meter dash. It's the third day of the games, the time is 14:30 and it's 31°C. You start in the fourth run. After 4 seconds you take over the runner-up and you keep that position. Which place did you reach?
Answer: 2

9) 15+8:(6*3-16)*(3+5-4)-(3*5*10)-(-19+6-6)=?
Solution = 9

10) How many sides does a tetrahedron have?
Answer: 4

11) In which quadrant of the coordinate system is 210° positioned??
Answer: 3

12) 518400 seconds = ? days
Answer: 6

13) A pool has a size of 6x4m and is 2.5m deep. How many cubic meters does it have?
Answer: 60

14) $$\frac{10^3 - 10^2 + 10^4 - 10^1 - 8*10^2 - 9*10^2}{5*10^3} = ?$$ Solution = 2

15)

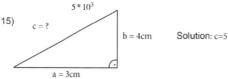

$c = ?$ $b = 4cm$ Solution: c=5
$a = 3cm$

16) $$\frac{R*B - (a+b)*N + B*N + (a+b) + N}{B*R - 2*(x+y) - (a+b) - 2} = 5$$

(a+b) = 5 = R
(x+y) = 4 = B
(c+d) = 2 = N

17) $$\frac{(^{625}\!/_{\%} -100+^{20}\!/_{10}) *6F}{^{3600}\!/_{600}} = 6$$

Schnüffel
KRIMINALFALL

ATTACHMENT CRIME NOVEL

Please laminate and cut into puzzle pieces

A mentally ill woman was stalking him.

afraid, because this woman was dangerous and not to be trusted.

Nobody believed him because the woman seemed harmless.

Schnüffel KRIMINALFALL

ATTACHEMENT CARDS

Please laminate and cut out

Richard Nebelhaus was struck dead with a log of wood

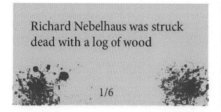

1/6

The latest crime novel, that Richard was working on, was stolen

4/6

The victim had large wounds on the back of the head, the forehead and the temple

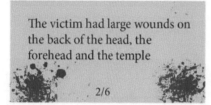

2/6

Richard has been dead for 10 days already

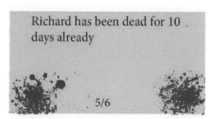

5/6

The cabin clearly shows signs of a struggle. Richard tried to fight off his killer

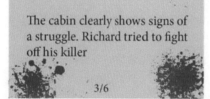

3/6

All valuables and money were left behind

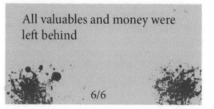

6/6

That was a sniff in the dark.

Go on sniffing and you will find something.

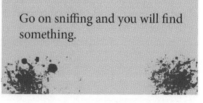

Unfortunately, you didn't sniff anything out.

Go on sniffing and you will be successful.

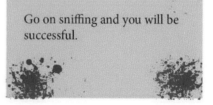

Schnüffel
KRIMINALFALL

Richard is single and has a 32-year-old son from his first marriage, named Rafael

1/7

Richard has no family and no siblings

2/7

5 weeks ago the victim retreated to the remote cabin to finish his latest crime novel

3/7

The author only has one close friend: the restaurant's owner Hannes Pflügl

4/7

Richard does not have a lot of contact with his son Rafael

5/7

Richards's crime novels are always based on a tiny little bit of truth. That's why they are so successful

6/7

The victim was known to be hardheaded, easily confused and often withdrawn

7/7

That was a sniff in the dark.

Go on sniffing and you will find something.

Unfortunately, you didn't sniff anything out.

Go on sniffing and you will be successful.

Richard's son resents his father, because he walked out on him and his mother years ago

1/6

The author has one big competitor: Markus Wilming, who loves stealing his ideas or copying them

4/6

Richard's ex-wife has psychological problems and has been in therapy for years.

2/6

The victim wasn't very well liked in the town he lived in due to his bizarre behavior.

5/6

Richard's ex-wife claims that she only started having mental problems once he left her.

3/6

Richard was always picking fights with everyone, hence he didn't have many friends.

6/6

That was a sniff in the dark.

Go on sniffing and you will be successful.

Go on sniffing and you will find something.

Unfortunately, you didn't sniff anything out.

Recently Verena had a lot of visits by a person whose identity is unknown.

1/5

Verena was clearly still in love with Richard.

4/5

She was prescribed stronger medication due to the fact that she still firmly believed that Richard and her were a couple.

2/5

The patient was in denial about the breakup with Richard

5/5

During her drugged-out haze she stated that Richard needed to be warned.

3/5

That was a sniff in the dark.

Go on sniffing and you will be successful.

Go on sniffing and you will find something.

Unfortunately, you didn't sniff anything out.

Schnüffel
KRIMINALFALL

Richard's ex-wife was in a mental institution when the murder took place.

1/5

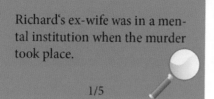

On the day of the murder Richard's ex-wife was on leave

2/5

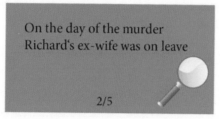

Richard's son Rafael was travelling abroad for business

3/5

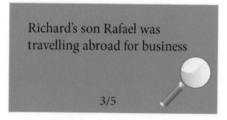

Rafael's business trip can be confirmed with the airline.

4/5

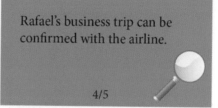

Markus Wilming, Richard's biggest competition, was on a book tour to introduce his lat[est] book.

5/5

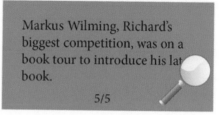

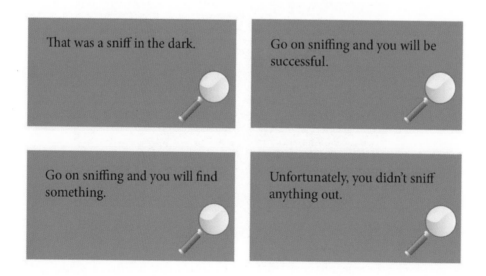

That was a sniff in the dark.

Go on sniffing and you will be successful.

Go on sniffing and you will find something.

Unfortunately, you didn't sniff anything out.

Schnüffel
KRIMINALFALL

ID'S

Please fill in names, laminate and cut out

Badge number.: 08990

_____

_____

with a license to sniff

certified

Badge number.: 08994

_____

_____

with a license to sniff

certified

Badge number.: 08991

_____

_____

with a license to sniff

certified

Badge number.: 08995

_____

_____

with a license to sniff

certified

Badge number.: 08992

_____

_____

with a license to sniff

certified

Badge number.: 08996

_____

_____

with a license to sniff

certified

Badge number.: 08993

_____

_____

with a license to sniff

certified

Badge number.: 08997

_____

_____

with a license to sniff

certified

Schnüffel
KRIMINALFALL

ATTACHEMENT PHOTO OF RICHARDS SON, BORN OUT OF WEDLOCK

Please laminate and cut out

ATTACHEMENT PUZZLE

Please laminate and cut into pieces